OUR PUPPET ECONOMY

By

Dennis Avola

PLAYBILL®

Our Puppet Economy

Puppet Characters

Mr. Gross Domestic Product (GDP) – *The Bodybuilder*

US Dollar Index Puppet – *Stars & Stripes Man*

The Inflation Puppet - *The Sun*

The Money Supply Puppet – *Fat Albert Person*

The Unemployment Puppet – *The Billboard*

The Puppeteers

The Federal Reserve Bank

The United States Treasury Department

<u>Traffic Lights on the Stage (Green or Red Light)</u>

The Federal Fund Interest Rate – *The interest rate established by the Federal Reserve is typically an overnight loan rate in which US banks borrow from other US Banks.*

Currency in Circulation – *The total value of US currency in the hands of the US Public*

M1 Deposit Reserve Rate – *The percentage of a Bank's deposits that are held by the Federal Reserve.*

Government Spending Rate – *The percentage growth of US federal & state government spending during a given time period.*

Personal Tax Rate – *The total household tax rate collected from income & spending.*

Corporate Tax Rate – *The total business tax rate on each dollar of profit.*

Everyone loves a good puppet show. As the puppet characters move and dance freely on their custom-built stage, we seem to ignore the attached strings and the clever hand movements made by the puppeteers. We are simply entertained as each puppet character is animated to tell us a story with the nimble movements of their legs and arms. There is little need for an audio track, only the auxiliary sounds that enhance the movement and actions of the puppets. The adeptness of the puppeteers is also transparent. And we soon believe that the puppet characters are real and acting on their own personal desires.

According to Wikipedia, "a puppet is an inanimate object or representational figure animated or manipulated by a puppeteer. The puppet undergoes a process of transformation through being animated and is normally manipulated by at least one puppeteer." How then is our economy like a puppet show?

The puppets representing our economy are inanimate characters, whereas its puppeteers are real people. Our puppeteers, the Federal Reserve Bank, and the US Treasury Department created a theatrical production by cleverly animating the puppet characters to tell a story of our economy. Ultimately, the audience watching the story unfold can better understand the cause and effect of changes to our economy from the actions taken by the puppeteers.

Each puppet character has a specific role on the stage. The gross domestic product (GDP) character, whose figure appears to look like a bodybuilder, moves about the stage as the puppet leader. The money supply puppet sitting in the corner of the stage eating a hotdog is clearly overweight but continues to ask for more. The US dollar puppet character acts like the host of the show, dressed in stars and stripe uniform that is perfectly tailored to his long, thin body type. The inflation puppet character, shaped like a balloon that expands and contracts, appears initially to be hiding from the audience, hanging from the stage ceiling, moving up and down and sideways without any restrictions. The last inanimate character on stage is the unemployment puppet who looks like a highway billboard with hands and feet, keeping score of the employment rate and informing the audience when it is intermission and time for the next act.

In front of the stage for the entire audience to view, there are six traffic-type lights that turn either green or red. Each traffic light is labelled accordingly, The Federal Fund Rate, the Currency in Circulation, Government Spending, Personal Taxes, Corporate Taxes, and the bank's Deposit Reserve Rate. These lights are controlled exclusively by the puppeteers, flashing green to show a positive or increasing change or red to show a decreasing change for each category they represent.

Three of the traffic lights, the Federal Fund Interest Rate, the Currency in Circulation, and the Bank's Deposit Reserve Rate, are monetary policy categories controlled by the Federal Reserve puppeteer. The remaining three traffic lights, Government Spending, Personal and Corporate Taxes, are fiscal policy categories controlled by the United States Treasury puppeteer. To animate our economy's puppets on stage, the puppeteers will turn the traffic lights to green or red to increase or decrease respectively one or more of the six monetary and fiscal policy categories to achieve their desired outcome for the economy.

The puppet show begins as the stage curtain is lifted slowly. All the puppet characters are on stage with the US Dollar character in his stars and strip uniform front and center, standing beside the GDP bodybuilder puppet character. The Money Supply puppet sitting in the corner of the stage is alongside the Unemployment character. Hanging from the stage rafters is the Inflation puppet.

The dangly puppet strings are visible as they connect their hands, feet, and mid-section to the puppeteer's hand controls. A trumpet sound starts the motion of the puppet characters.

The GDP puppet, flexing both of his biceps, takes a bow as the US Dollar character raises a poster sign for the audience to read, announcing the first act of the puppet show. It reads, 'Watch us grow our $28 Trillion economy in the United States'. Quickly, the US Treasury puppeteer goes to work by powering on the government spending light, turning it green for the audience to view. Soon, the smiling GDP puppet flexing his bicep muscles starts to grow taller and bigger as the audience watches with delight. The increasing government spending for infrastructure and military projects expands the output of goods and services in the economy, contributing to the GDP puppet's size and shape. In the corner of the stage, the Money Supply puppet shows his satisfaction by rubbing his bloated belly as the Federal Reserve puppeteer flashes red on its traffic light, lowering the economy's interest rate to borrow funds.

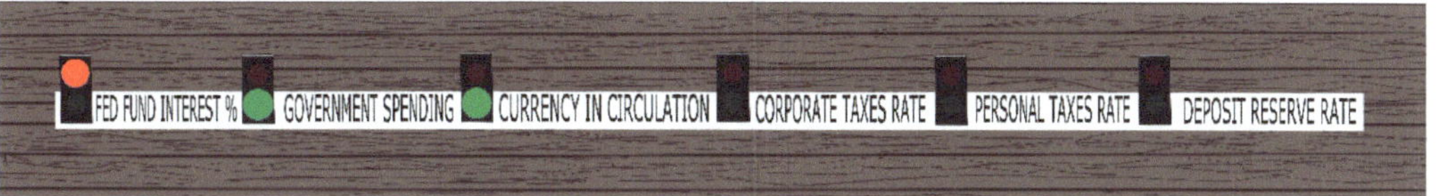

The perfect storm has been created with increased government spending for commercial infrastructure projects, like new roads and bridges, and new military production of aircraft and missiles, along with lower interest borrowing costs to fund these new economic output projects. The US economy is prepared for significant growth.

Swinging from the stage rafters, the Inflation puppet character starts to lower himself enough so that the audience becomes more aware of his presence. Still the Federal Reserve puppeteer keeps its traffic light in the red, indicating that its interest rate will remain low. And the US Treasury puppeteer keeps its government spending light on green, indicating new infrastructure, military, and household healthcare project spending. As a result, the Currency in Circulation traffic light has turned green indicating that the availability of money has increased in the economy. The US Treasury and Federal Reserve puppeteers agree to increase the printing of new fiat money to sustain their respective growth strategies which results in more currency in circulation. And the Money Supply puppet is happier getting exactly what he wanted more food. Plus, the GDP puppet loves it too as more, less costly funds are available. However, the US Dollar puppet starts to limp around with his head down as he paces the stage. More money in the economy lowers the value of the US dollar. Now the Inflation puppet in full view of the audience starts to reflect a bright glow over the stage characters. Something is happening as the puppeteers instruct the orchestra to play a soft melody so not to concern its apprehensive viewers.

The Unemployment billboard puppet character standing in the back of the stage starts to walk towards the front preparing to announce something to the audience. The trumpets play in the background as the Unemployment puppet holds up a poster sign that reads, America's unemployment rate has declined significantly. At the same time, the US Dollar puppet moves to the back of the stage taking a seat with his head down and elbows on his knees. He is debased, feeling less valuable as more money in the economy has lowered the exchange value of the US Dollar. But the stage has gotten much brighter as the Inflation puppet has grown larger and brighter. Suddenly, the GDP puppet starts to struggle with the Inflation puppet who is taking center control of the stage.

The stage's lights slowly darken and then brighten several times to reflect the passing of time. With the Inflation puppet remaining bright in the center of the stage, the stage's lights are finally switched on indicating that our puppet show has resumed with all the puppet characters. However, there is a different mood amongst the characters as they are standing spaces apart from each other. No one seems happy except for the Inflation puppet who now dominates the stage.

Our puppeteers sense the conflicts brewing on the stage between the US Dollar, the Inflation and GDP puppet characters. They quickly turn off the Federal Fund Interest Rate traffic light signaling that interest rates have stopped declining. However, the Currency in Circulation and the Government Spending traffic lights stay green indicating the continuance of printing new money and spending on new infrastructure, Military, and household social programs.

The US Dollar puppet raises his head up as he notices that the Federal Fund Interest Rate traffic light has been turned off. The Money Supply puppet raises both of his arms above his head making a jester of approval as he recognizes that the money printing press has not stopped creating new money for the continuance of government spending. However, our Inflation puppet remains bright, emitting a glow from the middle of the stage.

Soon, the Unemployment puppet walks across the front of the stage holding a poster sign reading that consumers and businesses have reduced their spending because of the higher inflationary prices in the marketplace and supply chain. With the Government Spending traffic light still shining green, our puppeteers decide to switch on the Federal Fund Interest Rate traffic light to green indicating an increase in interest rates for the economy. The Currency in Circulation traffic light is then turned off indicating that the money printing presses have been rolled back. The puppeteer's goal is to strengthen the US

Dollar puppet that has grown weak and non-responsive. With a stronger US Dollar, imported products will be less expensive and consumers may start buying again. The puppeteers also hope that the higher interest rates and a stronger US Dollar will encourage international countries to invest more in their puppet economy funding the growing spending budget of the US Government. With a stronger US Dollar, the economy's exports become more expensive hopefully offset by lower import product prices. Regardless, the economy's trade balance is affected by a stronger US Dollar and higher interest rates. The puppeteers must consider the importance of growing its home economy versus its trade balance with other countries.

With higher interest costs and inflated supply chain costs, the production output of the business community has started to contract. The Unemployment puppet then walks back across the stage holding a poster sign that reads the unemployment rate has increased while business output has slowed.

The inflation puppet remains bright, but the Money Supply puppet raises his hands to encourage the puppeteers to turn on the Currency in Circulation traffic light to green wanting more available money in the economy. In the foreground, the GDP bodybuilder puppet is lifting weights and appears happy and content with the Government Spending traffic light remaining green, even thou households and businesses have reduced their spending. The stage's lights then begin to darken and then brighten again several times to illustrate the passing of time.

The stage now takes on a different look. Our puppets who had been center stage when the show began, are now in the foreground standing around waiting for the puppeteers to pull their strings. The Inflation puppet has not moved back up to the stage rafters and still shines brightly. The Unemployment puppet continues to pace the stage communicating that the economy's unemployment rate continues to increase with selected industries. Nevertheless, our puppeteers continue to leave the Government Spending traffic light on green making the GDP puppet content, but the other puppets are now sitting in the corner of the stage watching each other to see what the puppeteers will do next.

The audience has witnessed a transformation on stage. An expanding economy has become burdened with a stronger US Dollar resulting from interest rate increases, slower GDP growth due to the higher cost of borrowing, an over-inflated money supply from prior money printing expansion and easy money loaning policies, and unemployment level starting to increase. However, inflation remains an ongoing issue. The puppeteers once again instruct the orchestra to play a soft melody so not to concern its apprehensive viewers. The melody represents the media's influence on the economy as the stage curtain is lower.

Reducing Inflation becomes the primary objective of the puppeteers. Their goal is to reduce inflation without causing a dramatic decline in GDP output (avoiding a recession) and maintain a stable unemployment rate in the economy. Whereas the Federal Reserve puppeteer has been funding the economy's growth plans for the US Treasury puppeteer with low borrowing interest rates and printing large volumes of currency, the puppeteers now need to work together to achieve their new goals while lowering inflation.

The stage curtain is lifted, and all the puppet characters are on stage facing the audience. However, the Inflation puppet is shining brightly in the middle of the stage above the other puppet characters.

There are many interrelationships between the puppet characters on stage. The US Dollar puppet is affected by the value of the Federal Reserve Interest Rate and the growth of the Money Supply in the economy, assuming no other changes in the global exchange market. As the Federal Fund Interest Rate is reduced (red traffic light), the US Dollar is weakened. Or when the value of the Money Supply grows, the US Dollar is further reduced making it less valuable compared to other major international currencies. But, with a weak US Dollar, our economy's exports will increase, creating more employment, income, and consumption. However, a weak US Dollar also makes imported products more expensive in the US Economy. And given our high consumption of imported products, we can expect the inflation puppet to grow bigger and brighter.

Our puppeteers have created an expanding economy by growing the money supply with low-interest rates that soon became over-inflated and started to contract as inflation took center stage. Our puppeteers, the Federal Reserve and the US Treasury, elected to continue to increase government expenditures for military, COVID, Infrastructure and other spending projects with the goal of stimulating the economy's output, GDP, which would lead to more employment, income, and consumption. However, this approach backfired as households and businesses began to reduce their purchasing patterns due to higher costs of goods and services. So, our puppeteers scheduled a meeting to discuss and change their strategy so to return the economy to its original scenario as depicted in the opening act of the puppet show.

The puppeteer's new goals for our puppet economy were to:

➢ Continue to grow the economy's output, GDP.

➢ Reduce the unemployment rate with the creation of new domestic jobs,

➢ Decrease and stabilize price inflation and

➢ Strengthen the US Dollar.

The banking system's money supply is the focal point of the economy controlled and managed by the Federal Reserve, the economy's central bank. The money supply consists of deposits made by US businesses, households, and international organizations. Businesses deposit their cash flow from profits, households deposit their income and savings, and international organizations make investments in our US banking system. In addition, the US Treasury can print fiat money currency as specified by the Federal Reserve which is distributed throughout the banking system as our economy's money supply. As the banking system lends out its money supply to businesses for expansion and households for buying homes, cars, etc., and for government spending programs the value of our money supply increases significantly as these loans get redeposited until the money is used, creating new, additional loans from this expanding money supply. This is called multiple deposit creation. So, our Money Supply puppet on stage sits contently getting fatter and fatter. If government spending increases, the economy's money supply must increase whereas the Federal Reserve puppeteer may inject funds into the economy's money supply to maintain the necessary funds for expanding government spending projects, like infrastructure, military, and social programs.

The trigger that grows the economy's money supply is the market interest rate established by the Federal Reserve puppeteer. Declining interest rates motivate spending by businesses, households, and government agencies. Spending drives the economy's output, which in turn reduces unemployment. With more employed workers, income and spending will increase proportionally. However, the value of the US dollar will weaken as interest rates are lower, assuming no other changes in the global exchange market as the economy's money supply increases. Therefore, our puppeteers have a challenge to restore the value of the US Dollar while stabilizing price inflation and keeping the economy's output (GDP) growing with low unemployment.

The puppeteers agree on the following strategy:

1. Increase the market interest rate (Federal Fund Rate) to slow down spending demand by businesses, households, and government agencies which in turn over time will reduce price inflation. The value of the US Dollar will also strengthen, assuming other global exchanges do not change. A stronger US Dollar will also contribute to lower-priced imported goods which in turn over time, will further reduce price inflation. Our inflation puppet should start to retreat from the center of the stage back to the rafters.

2. Reduce the government spending rate on infrastructure, military, and other social programs to reduce spending demand. Whereas this reduction in output will impact the economy's GDP, the goal would be getting individual businesses and newly created

small businesses to create more output with tax incentives.

3. Lower Corporate Taxes so that businesses will have an incentive to increase output and hiring. Lowering the unemployment rate will provide more income for household spending which accounts for about 70% of the economy's GDP.

The stage's lights then begin to darken and then brighten again several times to illustrate the passing of time. As the stage curtains are lifted again, the puppet characters on the stage have changed reflecting the positive outcome of the puppeteer's new economic policy strategies.

The Money supply puppet has stopped eating, showing that he has lost some weight. The US Dollar puppet is stronger now that the Federal Fund Interest rate has increased relative to the other global exchange rates, moving back to the front of the stage with more confidence. Our GDP puppet, Mr. GDP, remains positive showing his strength to maintain strong throughout the economic turmoil. And our unemployment puppet reports that the corporate tax reductions have created new jobs, lowering the economy's unemployment rate. In the end, our Inflation puppet has moved back up to the stage rafters reduced in size but still visible to the audience.

The puppet show has now ended as all the puppet characters come to the front of the stage, bowing to the audience. Our puppeteers, the Federal Reserve Bank and the US Treasury, then appear with their puppet characters, taking a bow to the audience.

Our puppet economy closes as the curtain closes on the stage. The audience has learned the significance of the puppeteers in controlling our economy.